THE CUSTOMER CODE

Secrets to Find, Attract and Keep Customers for Life

Falilat Adeyemi-Salami

Copyright © 2024 by Falilat Adeyemi-Salami

Published by

Mind2Global
mind2globaloasis@gmail.com

All rights reserved.

This publication is designed to provide accurate and authoritative information regarding the subject matter covered. It is sold with the understanding that the publisher does not render legal, accounting, or other professional services. If legal advice or other expert assistance is required, the services of a competent professional should be sought.

No part of this publication may be reproduced, stored in a retrieval system, or transmitted in whole or in part, in any form or by any means, electronic, mechanical, photocopying, recording, or otherwise, without the author's or the publisher's prior written permission.

For speaking engagements and bulk purchase, please contact the author on:

Table of Contents

Introduction IV

Part One

Staying Top Of The Customer's Mind 1

Chapter 1: Who Is A Customer? 2
- THE VITAL ROLE OF CUSTOMERS IN BUSINESS 2
- KEY QUESTIONS FOR IDENTIFYING CUSTOMERS 5
- KEY TAKEAWAYS FOR YOUR BRAND 12

Chapter 2: What Is Customer Service? 14
- THE POWER OF POSITIVE CUSTOMER EXPERIENCES 16
- PRACTICAL APPLICATIONS OF CUSTOMER SERVICE 20
- EVALUATING YOUR CUSTOMER SERVICE 20
- BUILDING A CUSTOMER-CENTRIC BUSINESS 21

Chapter 3: Why Offer Excellent Customer Services 23
- THE BENEFITS OF EXCELLENT CUSTOMER SERVICE 24

Chapter 4: Mindset Hacks For Great Customer Service Delivery 32

Chapter 5: Simple Reasons Customers Buy And Come Back 42
- WHY DO CUSTOMERS BUY AND RETURN? 42
- IMPLEMENTING SYSTEMS FOR ENHANCED CUSTOMER SERVICE 46
- CASE STUDIES: REAL-WORLD EXAMPLES OF EXCELLENT CUSTOMER SERVICE 50

Chapter 6: Twelve (12) Best Ways To Keep Customers Coming Back 53
- WHY KNOWING YOUR CUSTOMERS IS IMPORTANT 54
- HOW TO ENSURE SERVICE EXCELLENCE 61
- STRATEGIES FOR SHOWING APPRECIATION 65
- STRATEGIES FOR SEEKING AND ACTING ON FEEDBACK 68
- IMPORTANCE OF CONTINUOUS TRAINING 72
- STRATEGIES FOR EFFECTIVE TRAINING 73

Part Two

Understanding Customer-Specific Needs And Trigger Moments . 80

Chapter 7: Know Your Customer Journey 81

MAPPING OUT THE CUSTOMER JOURNEY AND TOUCHPOINTS......... 81
IDENTIFYING AND ENHANCING TOUCHPOINTS 85

Chapter 8 88

Address Their Pain Points And Opportunity For Improvement .. 88

STEP 1: GATHER FEEDBACK FROM CUSTOMERS 88
STEP 2: ANALYZE CUSTOMERS' FEEDBACK 89
STEP 3: PRIORITIZE IMPROVEMENTS 90
STEP 4: DEVELOP A PLAN OF ACTION 91
STEP 5: COMMUNICATE WITH CUSTOMERS 92
THE BENEFITS OF ADDRESSING PAIN POINTS AND IDENTIFYING
OPPORTUNITIES 92

Chapter 9 94

Handling Customer Trigger Moments 94

IDENTIFYING TRIGGER MOMENTS... 94
GATHERING DATA 95
SEGMENTING CUSTOMERS 96
DEVELOPING A PLAN OF ACTION 97
IMPLEMENTING AND EVALUATING 97
HANDLING CUSTOMER ANGER 98

Chapter 10 100

Types Of Customer Anger And Potential Ways To Address Them
.. 100

FRUSTRATION 100
BLAME 103
OUTRAGE 104
THE IMPACT ON BUSINESS... 107

Epilogue 108

Summary Of The Customer Code... 108

Call To Action. 112

Meet The Author 113

INTRODUCTION

It pains me to see businesses struggle, especially when the cause is a lack of basic customer service skills.

Imagine calling a company to complain and getting passed around with no solution. How would you feel as the customer? Yet, we see thriving companies and wonder how they do it. The answer is simple: they invest in basic customer service skills.

Keeping customers satisfied helps an organization build a valuable reputation for dependability and quality performance. Service-based interactions directly influence how customers perceive the product, service, and company. It is crucial to help employees develop service strategies that create a positive image, communicate effectively, and build customer rapport to support the organization's core values.

Why do some companies get more patronage than others? Why do you talk so much about a particular company and avoid others? What is the role of word of mouth in business? How do customer service skills affect a company's revenue? How can a company improve its customer service skills?

Every interaction with a customer is an opportunity to create a loyal advocate or a dissatisfied critic. Companies that understand this focus on training employees to handle complaints empathetically, resolve issues promptly, and go above and beyond to meet customer needs. They know that a happy customer is not only likely to return but also to spread positive feedback, bringing in more business.

This book will teach the essential qualities needed to keep customers returning and help participants develop a customer-centric attitude. It aims to equip you with the tools to transform your business by focusing on excellent customer service.

You'll learn how to:

- Implement practical strategies for effective communication and problem-solving.

- Build strong relationships with customers through personalized service.

- Create a culture of continuous improvement in customer service within your organization.

- Leverage customer feedback to enhance service delivery and product offerings.

- Understand the financial impact of superior customer service and how it contributes to long-term success.

Whether you're a small business owner, a customer service manager, or an employee on the front lines, this book will provide you with actionable insights and real-world examples to elevate your customer service skills. By mastering these principles, you'll improve customer satisfaction and drive growth and profitability for your business.

Read on to discover the secrets to finding, attracting, and keeping customers for life.

PART ONE

STAYING TOP OF THE CUSTOMER'S MIND

Chapter 1

WHO IS A CUSTOMER?

A customer is an individual, business, or organization that receives or purchases goods or services from another business. They are the cornerstone of any business, as they are the ones who ultimately generate revenue and profit. Understanding who your customers are and how to engage with them effectively is crucial for any business's success.

A customer, often referred to as a buyer or client, is someone who has the power to choose between different products and suppliers. This ability to choose makes it imperative for businesses to focus on providing exceptional products and services to attract and retain customers. The end user of these goods or services is known as the consumer.

The Vital Role of Customers in Business

Customers are the lifeblood of any business. Without them, no business can survive or thrive.

They aren't just people who buy stuff—they play several key crucial roles for any business to succeed. Here are some of the key roles they play in making your business successful:

1. Source of Revenue

First and foremost, customers are the ones who bring in the money. Their purchases are what keep the business running. A business simply can't make money without customers buying products or services.

2. Feedback Providers

Customers are great at telling you what's working and what isn't. Through reviews, surveys, or even casual conversations, they give you feedback that can help you improve your products or services. Listening to them can help you make better decisions.

3. Brand Advocates

Happy customers often tell their friends and family about your business. This word-of-mouth is incredibly powerful and can help you attract new customers without spending much on advertising. Essentially, your satisfied customers become your best marketers.

4. Loyalty Contributors

When customers keep coming back, they provide a steady stream of revenue. Loyal customers are gold—they're more likely to buy again and even spend more over time. Keeping them happy is key to long-term success.

5. Market Influencers

Customers can influence market trends. Their preferences and buying habits shape what products or services become popular. By paying attention to what they want, businesses can stay ahead of the competition and adapt to changes in the market.

6. Service Quality Evaluators

Customers judge the quality of your service. Positive experiences lead to repeat business, while negative ones can harm your reputation. Ensuring good service is crucial for maintaining customer trust and loyalty.

7. Purchasing Decision Drivers

Customers' choices determine what products or services are successful. Their buying decisions influence which items stay on the market and which don't. Understanding their preferences helps businesses tailor their offerings to meet demand.

8. Community Builders

Customers can create a community around your brand. Whether through social media, events, or other engagement activities, they help build a network of loyal supporters. This community can be a powerful tool for marketing and fostering brand loyalty.

In short, customers are much more than just buyers—they're the driving force behind any successful business. By recognizing and valuing their different roles, businesses can improve their strategies, enhance customer satisfaction, and achieve lasting growth.

Key Questions for Identifying Customers

To successfully identify your customers, you need to ask critical questions that help you understand who they are, what they need, and how best to reach them. Here are some essential questions to guide this process:

1. Who are our potential customers?

- What are their demographics (age, gender, income level, education, occupation)?
- Where do they live (location, urban vs. rural)?
- What is their lifestyle like (hobbies, interests, values)?

2. What problems do they face that our product/service can solve?

- What specific pain points or challenges do they experience?
- How does our product or service address these issues?
- What benefits do they seek from a solution?

3. How do they currently solve these problems?

- What alternatives or competitors do they use?

- What do they like or dislike about these existing solutions?
- How often do they purchase products or services like ours?

4. What motivates their purchasing decisions?

- What factors are most important to them (price, quality, convenience, brand reputation)?
- What triggers them to make a purchase (seasonal needs, personal milestones, external events)?
- How do they make buying decisions (impulse purchases, planned buying, influenced by others)?

5. Where do they gather information and make purchases?

- Which online platforms and social media do they use?
- Do they prefer shopping online or in physical stores?
- What sources do they trust for recommendations and reviews?

6. How can we best communicate with them?

- What type of content resonates with them (informative, entertaining, emotional)?

- What communication channels do they prefer (email, social media, direct mail, in-store)?
- How often do they want to hear from us?

7. What are their expectations and preferences?

- What level of customer service do they expect?
- How do they prefer to receive support (phone, chat, email, self-service)?
- What kind of post-purchase engagement do they value (follow-up emails, loyalty programs, feedback opportunities)?

8. How can we build and maintain a relationship with them?

- What keeps them returning (rewards programs, personalized offers, excellent customer service)?
- How do they want to be recognized and valued as loyal customers?
- What kind of community or social engagement do they appreciate?

9. What are their future needs and trends?

- How might their needs evolve over time?
- What emerging trends could influence their behavior?
- How can we anticipate and adapt to these changes?

10. What does our ideal customer look like?

- How can we define our target customer profile based on the above insights?

- Which customer segments are most profitable and aligned with our business goals?

- How can we prioritize our efforts to attract and retain these ideal customers?

By addressing these questions, businesses can create a detailed and accurate profile of their target customers, leading to more effective marketing strategies, better product development, and, ultimately, higher customer satisfaction and loyalty.

Categorizing Customers

A business is defined by its customers, who can be categorized into three major groups:

1. **Past Customers**
2. **Present Customers**
3. **Potential Customers**

Past Customers are those who have had a previous buying relationship with a business. They provide valuable insights into customer loyalty and satisfaction. Engaging with past customers can lead to repeat business and referrals.

Present Customers are those who have purchased or used a business product within a designated period and continue to do so. They are the backbone of a business's current revenue stream. Ensuring these customers are satisfied and loyal is crucial for maintaining a steady income and fostering word-of-mouth recommendations.

Potential Customers are those who are yet to buy but will eventually become buyers. This category is an ideal market for a business consisting of observers of previous and present customers. They are influenced by the experiences and reviews of others, making them a crucial target for marketing efforts.

Importance of Understanding Customer Categories

Understanding these categories helps businesses tailor their strategies to engage each group effectively. By paying attention to the needs and behaviors of past, present, and potential customers, businesses can deepen existing relationships and reach untapped consumer populations, increasing traffic and sales.

Here's why it matters:

1. Personalized Marketing

Categorizing customers allows businesses to tailor marketing efforts to specific groups. Personalized marketing messages are more likely to resonate with customers, leading to higher engagement and conversion rates. For instance, a business can send targeted promotions to high-value customers while offering introductory discounts to new customers.

2. Improved Customer Experience

When businesses understand the different categories of their customers, they can better anticipate and meet their needs. This leads to a more satisfying customer experience, enhancing loyalty and encouraging repeat business. For example, offering premium services to VIP customers or providing more educational content to new users can significantly improve their experience.

3. Efficient Resource Allocation

By identifying customer categories, businesses can allocate resources more efficiently. This ensures that marketing budgets, customer service efforts, and product development resources are directed where they will have the most impact. For instance, investing more in retaining high-value customers rather than spreading resources thinly across all segments.

4. Product and Service Development

Understanding customer categories helps businesses develop products and services that better meet the specific needs of each group. This can lead to innovation and improved offerings that attract and retain customers. For example, a company might develop a premium product version for one segment and a budget-friendly version for another.

5. Enhanced Customer Retention

Different customer categories have different retention needs. By understanding these, businesses can implement targeted retention strategies. For instance, loyal customers might appreciate loyalty programs, while new customers might need onboarding support to understand the product's or service's value.

6. Better Market Segmentation

Customer categorization is a crucial aspect of market segmentation. It allows businesses to divide their market into segments based on specific criteria like demographics, buying behavior, and preferences. This enables more precise targeting and positioning of products and services.

7. Insightful Analytics and Reporting

Categorizing customers enhances the quality of data analytics. It provides deeper insights into customer behavior, preferences, and trends. Businesses can track the performance of different customer segments and make data-driven decisions to optimize their strategies.

8. Strategic Planning

Understanding customer categories is crucial for long-term strategic planning. It helps businesses forecast demand, plan for future growth, and align their business goals with customer needs. For example, recognizing a growing segment of eco-conscious consumers can drive a company to adopt more sustainable practices.

9. Competitive Advantage

Businesses that effectively categorize and understand their customers can gain a competitive edge. They are better equipped to meet customer needs, adapt to market changes, and differentiate themselves from competitors. This leads to stronger customer relationships and a more loyal customer base.

10. Customer Lifetime Value Optimization

Different customer categories have varying lifetime values. By understanding these categories, businesses can focus on maximizing the lifetime value of each segment. This might involve investing more in high-value customers or developing strategies to increase the value of lower-value segments.

Understanding customer categories enables businesses to deliver personalized experiences, allocate resources efficiently, develop better products and services, and ultimately, build stronger customer relationships. This comprehensive approach drives customer satisfaction, loyalty, and long-term business success.

Key Takeaways for Your Brand

Think of your brand service areas and how you are ensuring good service at every touch point. Are you effectively engaging with your past, present, and potential customers? Are you actively seeking and acting on customer feedback? Are you building a culture that prioritizes customer satisfaction? By addressing these questions, you can create a strategy that ensures your customers are satisfied and loyal, ultimately leading to the success and growth of your business.

Chapter 2

WHAT IS CUSTOMER SERVICE?

So, what exactly is customer service? At its core, customer service is the process of ensuring satisfaction with a product or service. It involves the support provided before, during, and after a transaction, making the customer's experience as smooth and enjoyable as possible. This includes helping customers choose the right product, assisting with transactions, resolving issues, and providing ongoing support.

Customer service has evolved beyond the traditional model of telephone support. Today, it encompasses a variety of channels, including email, web chat, text messages, and social media. Many businesses also offer self-service options, allowing customers to find answers anytime. This multi-channel approach ensures that support is accessible and convenient, meeting customers where they are.

Understanding Customer Loyalty

Why do you choose one store over another repeatedly? Perhaps you've gone out of your way to purchase from a specific place, even when similar options are available closer to you. What makes you prefer one bank, brand, or supplier over another? Why do you stick with a particular mechanic for your car? The answers to these questions lie in the heart of customer service.

Customer loyalty isn't just about the product or service offered; it's deeply rooted in the experience customers have with a brand. When customers feel valued and understood, they are more likely to return. This emotional connection is what drives loyalty. Businesses that prioritize customer satisfaction and build strong relationships create a sense of trust and reliability.

Take, for example, a local coffee shop that remembers your name and favorite order. This personal touch can make a significant difference, transforming a routine transaction into a pleasant experience. Consistency in quality and service also plays a critical role. When customers know they can expect the same high standard every time they interact with your business, it reinforces their choice to stick with you.

Another key factor is how issues are handled. Even the best businesses encounter problems, but the response to these issues can make or break customer loyalty. Prompt, effective, and empathetic problem-solving shows customers that their concerns are taken seriously.

Moreover, customer loyalty programs that reward repeat business can enhance customers' sense of value and appreciation. These programs can range from simple point systems to more personalized rewards that reflect the preferences and behaviors of individual customers.

In essence, fostering customer loyalty requires a holistic approach. It's about creating positive experiences, maintaining consistency, handling problems with care, and showing genuine appreciation. When customers feel connected to your brand on multiple levels, they are likelier to remain loyal and even become advocates, bringing new customers through word-of-mouth.

The Power of Positive Customer Experiences

As consumers, we often become advocates for the businesses we frequent, not just because of the products they offer but because of how they make us feel. Poor service can drive us away from a company, no matter how good their products may be, and we might not only take our business elsewhere but also share our negative experiences with friends and colleagues, steering them away. On the other hand, good customer service fosters positive word-of-mouth brand loyalty, ultimately maximising profits. A business that excels in customer service can see significant growth in its revenue and overall success.

Positive experiences create emotional connections with customers. When customers feel valued and appreciated, they are more likely to return and recommend the business to others. This is why many successful companies invest heavily in training their staff to provide exceptional service. Employees who are empowered to go above and beyond for customers can turn ordinary interactions into memorable ones. Consider a scenario where a customer enters a store with a specific need. A well-trained employee helps them find what they're looking for and offers additional advice or suggestions that enhance their purchase. This level of personalised service leaves a lasting impression, making the customer feel understood and cared for.

Moreover, positive experiences can offset occasional negative ones. A loyal customer consistently receiving excellent service will likely overlook a rare mishap. This tolerance is built on the trust and satisfaction established over time. Conversely, a single negative experience in a sea of poor service can be the tipping point for customers to take their business elsewhere.

Investing in customer experience also has a quantifiable impact. Studies have shown that businesses with superior customer service outperform their competitors regarding profitability and market share. Satisfied customers are not just repeat buyers; they are also less price-sensitive, more willing to try new products, and more forgiving of mistakes. The rise of social media has amplified the impact of customer experiences. Positive reviews and testimonials shared online can reach a broad audience, acting as free marketing for the business. Conversely, negative reviews can spread just as quickly, highlighting the importance of consistently providing positive experiences.

Customer service is more than just a transaction; it is the ongoing process of ensuring customer satisfaction with a product or service. In today's world, customer service has evolved beyond traditional phone support and now includes various channels such as email, web, text messages, and social media. Many businesses also offer self-service options, allowing customers to find solutions anytime. Modern customer service is characterised by its multi-channel approach, where customers expect to interact with businesses through their preferred methods, whether quick text message exchanges, detailed emails, or real-time social media interactions. Self-service options such as comprehensive FAQs, online chatbots, detailed how-to guides, and videos have become increasingly popular. These resources empower customers to resolve issues independently, leading to faster resolutions and higher satisfaction rates, which enhance the customer experience and reduce the workload on customer service representatives, allowing them to focus on more complex issues.

Effective customer service is proactive rather than reactive, anticipating customer needs and addressing potential issues before they become problems. Proactive service demonstrates that a business values its customers' time and is committed to providing a smooth experience. The quality of customer service directly impacts a company's reputation. Exceptional service can differentiate a business in a crowded market, making it stand out as a preferred choice. Conversely, poor service can damage a brand's image and drive customers away. This is why businesses invest in training their customer service teams to handle interactions with empathy, patience, and efficiency.

Personalisation is another key aspect of modern customer service. Recognising and addressing customers by name, remembering their preferences, and tailoring recommendations based on past interactions can significantly enhance the customer experience. Personalised service makes customers feel valued and understood, fostering loyalty and encouraging repeat business.

Ultimately, the goal of any business should be to create a loyal customer base that feels genuinely connected to the brand. This requires a commitment to understanding and meeting customer needs, consistently delivering high-quality service, and creating positive interactions at every touchpoint. By focusing on these areas, businesses can ensure customer satisfaction, foster loyalty, and drive success, with outstanding customer service becoming a vital part of the brand promise. Companies that excel in customer service often see their customers doing the marketing for them through positive word of mouth, reducing the need for heavy marketing expenses. When customers feel valued and appreciated, they become advocates who drive the success and growth of the business.

Practical Applications of Customer Service

To illustrate the importance of customer service, consider the following scenarios:

1. **Personal Touch:** A local bakery remembers your favorite pastry and has it ready when you walk in. This personal attention makes you feel valued and encourages repeat visits.

2. **Efficient Problem Solving:** An online retailer quickly resolves an issue with your order, providing a refund or replacement without hassle. This efficient service builds trust and confidence in the brand.

3. **Proactive Support:** A software company sends helpful tips and updates to ensure you get the most out of their product. This proactive approach enhances your experience and increases the likelihood of renewal.

Evaluating Your Customer Service

Think about your brand and the service areas you offer. Evaluate how you ensure excellent service at every touchpoint. Consider the following questions:

- How do your employees interact with customers during sales and support interactions?

- What processes are in place to handle customer inquiries and complaints efficiently?

- How accessible is your customer support across different channels (phone, email, social media, etc.)?

- What measures are you taking to gather and act on customer feedback?

Building a Customer-Centric Business

For entrepreneurs and businesses, offering excellent customer service is a competitive advantage. Good locations, high-quality products, and skilled staff set a business apart. It's essential to provide consistent, high-quality service at every touchpoint, ensuring customers feel valued and supported throughout their journey.

Consider the following strategies to enhance customer service:

- **Training:** Invest in training programs for your staff to ensure they have the skills and knowledge to provide excellent service.

- **Feedback:** Regularly collect and analyze customer feedback to identify areas for improvement.

- **Technology:** Utilize technology to streamline support processes and make it easier for customers to get help.

- **Empathy:** Encourage a customer-first mindset, where staff prioritizes understanding and addressing customer needs.

Customer service is the backbone of any successful business. It's about resolving issues and creating positive experiences that build loyalty and drive growth. By prioritizing customer service, your business can differentiate itself in the competitive market, foster long-term relationships, and achieve sustainable success.

Chapter 3

WHY OFFER EXCELLENT CUSTOMER SERVICES

Excellent customer service is not merely a department within a business; it is a fundamental strategy that profoundly influences a company's success. In today's competitive market, outstanding customer service is essential for distinguishing your brand and creating lasting customer relationships.

The benefits of exceptional service range from increased revenue and reduced costs to enhanced customer loyalty and positive word-of-mouth marketing. By prioritizing superior customer service, businesses can track growth, identify improvement areas, address issues effectively, and constructively manage feedback.

This holistic approach ensures that customers remain satisfied, loyal, and willing to advocate for your brand, ultimately driving your business's long-term success and sustainability.

The Benefits of Excellent Customer Service

Offering outstanding customer service provides numerous benefits to a business. The payoff includes increased revenue, higher profit margins, reduced costs, and positive word-of-mouth advertising, which attracts more customers at a lower marketing cost.

Customer service is vital for retaining customers and extracting more value from them. Businesses can recover customer acquisition costs and build a loyal customer base by providing exceptional service. Loyal customers are likelier to refer friends and colleagues, provide testimonials, and write positive reviews. They also tend to be more understanding when issues arise and less sensitive to price increases.

Investing in customer service can significantly boost your business. Loyal customers can act as brand ambassadors, helping to acquire new customers more effectively than traditional marketing efforts. Here are some critical advantages of excellent customer service:

1. Customer Retention is Cheaper than Customer Acquisition

Increasing customer retention by just 5% can lead to a profit increase of at least 25%. Repeat customers tend to spend 67% more with your brand, reducing operating costs. Investing in customer service can lower your churn rate, thereby decreasing the amount spent on acquiring new customers and reducing the overall customer acquisition cost (CAC).

2. Customer Service Reflects Your Brand Image, Mission, and Values

Your customers form their perceptions of your brand based on your social media presence, advertisements, content, and customer service interactions. The customer service team is the primary link between your business and your customers, making it essential to convey your brand image and values. A well-trained customer service team can positively influence customers and highlight your strengths over competitors.

3. Happy Customers Will Refer Others

Satisfied customers are more likely to recommend your brand to friends, family, and coworkers. Research shows that 77% of customers have shared positive brand experiences with others. Excellent customer service leads to delighted customers who are more inclined to spread the word, providing the best and most cost-effective form of advertising.

4. Good Customer Service Encourages Loyalty

Customers with positive experiences with your brand are less likely to switch to competitors. Retaining existing customers is more cost-effective than acquiring new ones. Loyal customers generate higher lifetime value, increasing your company's profit. By offering stellar customer service, you can differentiate your company and build lasting relationships based on trust.

5. Addressing Customer Complaints Enhances Loyalty

Many customers do not complain because they believe it won't help or don't know where to complain. Unresolved dissatisfaction can lead to decreased loyalty. Customers who complain and have their issues resolved are more loyal than those who don't complain. Properly handling customer complaints can increase retention and reduce negative word-of-mouth, which travels faster than positive feedback.

6. Customers are Willing to Pay More for Better Service

Half of the customers are willing to increase their spending with a brand after a positive service experience. Moreover, 86% would pay up to 25% more for better customer service. In an era where businesses prioritize customer service, those that fail to do so risk losing customers to competitors. A single positive or negative experience can significantly influence a customer's loyalty.

7. Customer Service Employees Provide Valuable Insights

Understanding how customers perceive your brand is crucial. Your customer service team can gather insights directly from customer interactions, helping you align your marketing and product strategies with customer values. This ongoing feedback loop is essential for staying attuned to shifting customer trends and continuously improving your business.

Importance of Customer Service to Customers

For customers, excellent service is more than just a pleasant interaction; it is a significant factor in their overall experience and satisfaction with a brand. Regardless of the type of business, customers value being treated with respect, consideration, and care. Outstanding customer service makes customers feel valued, important, and heard, directly addressing their needs and ensuring their satisfaction. Here's why exceptional customer service is vital from the customer's perspective:

1. Feeling Loved and Cared For

Customers appreciate businesses that demonstrate genuine concern for their needs and well-being. When companies show empathy and go the extra mile to meet customer expectations, it fosters a sense of being valued. This can be as simple as a friendly greeting, personalized service, or follow-up communications to ensure satisfaction. Such gestures build trust and create emotional connections, encouraging customers to return and remain loyal.

Examples and Strategies:

- **Personalized Interactions:** Address customers by their names and remember their preferences.

- **Follow-ups:** Contact customers after a purchase or service to ensure everything is satisfactory.

- **Empathy:** Train staff to understand and respond to customer emotions and concerns effectively.

2. Feeling Important

Customers want to feel that they matter to the businesses they patronize. Offering thoughtful extras or exceeding expectations can significantly enhance their experience. This could be through small, unexpected gestures like complimentary services, personalized thank-you notes, or loyalty rewards. When customers feel important, they are more likely to develop a strong affinity for the brand and become repeat buyers.

Examples and Strategies:

- **Surprise and Delight:** Include a small gift or thank-you note with purchases.

- **Exclusive Offers:** Provide special deals or discounts to loyal customers.

- **Recognition Programs:** Acknowledge long-term customers or those who refer new clients.

3. Addressing Customer Pain Points

Effective customer service ensures customer complaints and issues are heard and resolved promptly. When businesses actively listen to and address customer concerns, it demonstrates that they value customer feedback and are committed to continuous improvement. This not only resolves the immediate problem but also prevents future issues and enhances the overall customer experience.

Examples and Strategies:

- **Accessible Support:** Offer multiple channels for customer support, such as phone, email, live chat, and social media.

- **Timely Responses:** Aim to resolve complaints quickly and efficiently.

- **Feedback Mechanisms:** Implement systems for gathering and acting on customer feedback.

4. Building Trust and Reliability

When customers receive consistent and reliable service, it builds trust. They know they can count on the business to meet their needs, which reduces anxiety and fosters a sense of security. Trust is a crucial component in customer loyalty and long-term relationships.

Examples and Strategies:

- **Consistency:** Ensure service quality is consistent across all touchpoints.

- **Transparency:** Communicate clearly about policies, procedures, and any changes that may affect customers.

- **Reliability:** Always deliver on promises and rectify mistakes promptly.

5. Enhancing Customer Experience

Excellent customer service significantly enhances the overall customer experience. Customers' positive interactions with a brand contribute to their overall perception and satisfaction. This holistic experience includes the product or service and the support and care they receive throughout their customer journey.

Examples and Strategies:

- **User-Friendly Processes:** Make it easy for customers to get help, make purchases, and find information.

- **Customer-Centric Culture:** Foster a culture within the business that prioritizes customer needs and satisfaction.

- **Continuous Improvement:** Regularly assess and improve customer service practices based on feedback and trends.

6. Creating Advocates

Satisfied customers are likely to become advocates for your brand. They share their positive experiences with friends, family, and colleagues, which can lead to new customer acquisitions through word-of-mouth referrals. By investing in excellent customer service, businesses can create a loyal customer base that actively promotes the brand.

Examples and Strategies:

- **Referral Programs:** Encourage satisfied customers to refer others by offering incentives.

- **Social Proof:** Share positive reviews and testimonials on your website and social media.

- **Community Engagement:** Engage with customers on social platforms and respond to their posts and reviews.

Investing in excellent customer service benefits both customers and businesses. From making customers feel valued and essential to addressing their concerns and enhancing their overall experience, outstanding service fosters loyalty and advocacy. These positive experiences not only retain customers but attract new ones, driving growth and success for the business. In the end, the value of excellent customer service extends far beyond individual transactions, creating a lasting impact on customer satisfaction and business reputation.

Chapter 4

MINDSET HACKS FOR GREAT CUSTOMER SERVICE DELIVERY

The kind of mindsets we have greatly influences how we handle customers. We need to adopt certain attitudes if we are genuinely concerned about delivering a great customer experience. Here are the essential mindsets to ensure outstanding customer service:

Mindset 1

You Can Afford to Be Generous

Before interacting with customers, believing that your business is secure and you have enough to share is crucial. Even if your business isn't booming now, projecting confidence is vital. Here's why this mindset matters:

Feeling Secure and Abundant

Imagine feeling like your business is on solid ground, even if it's not making huge profits. This sense of security allows you to be generous. Generosity means being willing to give a little extra to your customers without worrying too much about the immediate cost.

Examples of Generosity

Think of times when businesses have gone above and beyond for you:

- **Free Refills**: Like getting free refills on coffee or letting you use their restroom even if you're not buying anything.

- **Extra Service**: Provide extra milk and sugar or spend extra time answering all your questions thoroughly.

Contrast with Poor Service

Now, recall times when you felt disappointed as a customer:

- **Restrictive Policies**: Businesses that make you buy something to use their restroom or charge you extra for small things like sauce.

- **Unwelcoming Attitudes**: Salespeople who ignore you because they don't think you'll spend much.

Scarcity vs. Generosity Mindset

Bad service often comes from a scarcity mindset—fearing that every little expense will sink the business. This short-term thinking can prevent businesses from investing in long-term customer loyalty.

Benefits of Generosity

When you genuinely believe you can afford to be generous, it changes how you treat your customers:

- **Share and Be Nice**: Give refunds or take a small financial hit now for long-term gains.

- **Smart Business Move**: For example, losing money on something small like extra sauce can lead to a loyal customer who spends a lot over the years and tells others about your excellent service.

Having a mindset of abundance and generosity isn't just about being nice—it's a smart business strategy. It builds trust, loyalty, and positive word-of-mouth, which are priceless for any business. By feeling secure and willing to share a little extra, you create a customer experience that stands out and keeps people coming back.

This mindset benefits your customers and sets your business apart from others who operate from a place of fear and tight financial control.

Mindset 2

The Customer is More Important Than the Company

You weigh the pros and cons when making a big decision, like choosing between a higher-paying job with less freedom versus a lower-paying one with more freedom. Eventually, you prioritize what matters most to you—whether it's money or freedom.

In the context of customer service, you must decide upfront that your customers' happiness is the top priority, even if it means sacrificing some short-term gains in profitability. Here's why this mindset is crucial:

Customer Happiness Comes First

Just like how you prioritize your values in a job decision, in business, putting customers first means making decisions that prioritize their satisfaction over maximizing profits in every interaction.

Empowering Your Team

You can't oversee every decision in your company. Therefore, ensuring that every team member understands and embraces the value of prioritizing customer happiness is essential. They should know that whenever they have to make a decision, they should choose what's best for the customer's happiness, even if it doesn't immediately benefit the company financially.

Customer-Centric Culture

By establishing a customer-centric culture, where every employee knows that pleasing the customer is paramount, you create an environment where customers feel valued and respected. This approach builds loyalty and positive relationships.

Long-Term Benefits

While it might seem counterintuitive to prioritize customer happiness over immediate profits, satisfied customers are more likely to return and recommend your business to others in the long run. This word-of-mouth promotion can lead to sustainable growth and success.

Deciding that the customer is more important than the company involves setting a clear value system within your business. It means committing to prioritize customer happiness in every decision fostering a customer-centric culture throughout your organization. This approach enhances customer satisfaction and improves your business's long-term success and reputation. Making customers feel valued and prioritized lays the foundation for lasting relationships and sustainable business growth.

Mindset 3

Customer Service is a Profit Center

Companies often focus heavily on attracting new customers but sometimes neglect the importance of enhancing the customer experience after the initial sale.

While acquiring new customers is important, retaining existing customers is even more profitable in the long term. It's commonly said that acquiring a new customer is five times harder than retaining an existing one. Therefore, a wise business strategy is to keep your current customers satisfied.

Customer service should not be seen as merely an expense to be minimized. Instead, it should be considered a core part of your business strategy, akin to sales. By providing exceptional service, you enhance customer loyalty, increase repeat business, and stimulate positive word-of-mouth referrals.

To make customer service a profit center, hire and train employees who are not only skilled but also empathetic and personable. These employees should have the time and resources to dedicate themselves fully to customer interactions rather than rushing through them.

Ensure that your customers feel valued and cared for during every interaction. This can involve personalizing service, responding promptly to inquiries, and resolving issues effectively. When customers feel engaged and satisfied, they are likelier to remain loyal to your brand and recommend it to others.

While automation can streamline processes, ensure it doesn't detract from personalized customer service. Maintain a balance by having enough human interaction to address customer needs genuinely and empathetically.

Invest in customer service by scaling your team appropriately as your business grows. If communication with customers becomes too brief or impersonal due to workload, it's a sign that more staff may be needed to maintain high service standards.

Viewing customer service as a profit center means recognizing its pivotal role in maintaining customer satisfaction and driving long-term profitability. By prioritizing the customer experience and investing in skilled and dedicated personnel, businesses can foster loyalty, increase repeat business, and cultivate a positive reputation. This approach enhances financial returns and strengthens the business's overall resilience and growth potential in a competitive market.

Mindset 4

Every Interaction is a Moment to Shine

When customers reach out to your customer service team, it's a chance to make a significant impact.

Only a tiny percentage of your customers will directly interact with your customer service team. Therefore, each interaction is precious. It's an opportunity to go above and beyond, exceeding their expectations and showing them how much you value them.

Encourage your customer service representatives to spend a few extra minutes with each customer. Instead of rushing through the conversation to save time, they should focus on building rapport and deeply understanding the customer's needs. This personal touch makes customers feel valued and cared for.

By prioritizing meaningful interactions, you enhance the customer experience and create a positive work environment for your team. Encouraging employees to engage with customers personally fosters job satisfaction and pride in delivering exceptional service.

Creating Positive Outcomes

Investing time in each interaction can lead to numerous benefits:

- **Improved Customer Perception**: Customers appreciate genuine interest and care.

- **Enhanced Loyalty**: Positive interactions build trust and loyalty over time.

- **Positive Word-of-Mouth**: Satisfied customers are more likely to recommend your business to others.

Treating every interaction as a moment to shine isn't just about immediate satisfaction but building lasting relationships. Businesses that prioritize customer-centric interactions see higher retention rates and sustainable growth.

Mindset 5

Lose Every Fight

When a customer is upset, it's important to acknowledge their feelings and accept responsibility if the company is at fault. This approach prioritizes customer satisfaction over being right.

In situations with conflict, the goal is to ensure the customer feels heard and valued. Retaining the customer's trust and loyalty is a long-term benefit, even if it means conceding.

With social media and other digital platforms, customer interactions are often public. What you say and do can be seen by others, influencing your company's reputation. It's crucial to handle each situation with professionalism and integrity.

By addressing complaints effectively, you can turn dissatisfied customers into loyal advocates. Their positive experiences shared with others can significantly impact your business's reputation and growth.

Mindset 6

Rebelliously Right the Wrongs of the World

Rather than conforming to industry standards, dare to challenge them. Identify common practices that frustrate customers and innovate by offering better solutions.

Your business is an opportunity to demonstrate how things can be done better. Whether improving service quality or setting higher ethical standards, be a leader in your industry.

Taking a rebellious approach can be motivating, both for your team and your customers. It shows confidence in your convictions and a commitment to doing what's right, not just what's typical.

Standing out by doing things differently can attract attention and loyalty from customers who appreciate your unique approach. It sets your business apart and can lead to long-term success and growth.

Adopting these mindsets will transform how you and your team handle customer service. By cultivating a sense of generosity, prioritizing customer happiness, treating customer service as a profit center, shining in every interaction, letting customers win, and rebelliously righting the wrongs of the world, you'll create a business known for its outstanding customer experience. This approach benefits your customers and ensures long-term success and profitability for your company.

Chapter 5

SIMPLE REASONS CUSTOMERS BUY AND COME BACK

Customer service is a critical element that can make or break a business. The mindset behind delivering exceptional customer service is rooted in understanding why customers buy and why they return. Achieving this isn't about magic, trickery, or sheer luck. It is about creating systems that enhance customer service and loyalty.

Why Do Customers Buy and Return?

Customers choose to buy from and return to a business for several reasons. These reasons are often tied to how well the business meets their expectations and addresses their needs. Below are some key factors that influence customer decisions to stay loyal to a brand.

1. Clear Brand Promises and Consistent Delivery

One of the foremost expectations customers have is that a business will deliver on its brand promises. When a business promotes values such as reliability, excellence, and consistency, customers expect these qualities to be evident in every interaction and transaction.

Consistency is particularly crucial. Customers want to know that they can rely on a business to deliver the same high-quality service or product every time they engage with it. For example, a business must consistently provide timely responses and deliveries if it promises fast service. Inconsistent experiences can lead to disappointment and loss of trust.

Brand uniqueness also plays a role. When a business stands out for its unique qualities and consistently delivers on its promises, it gives customers a compelling reason to remain loyal. Whether through exceptional customer service, superior product quality, or innovative solutions, businesses that consistently meet or exceed their brand promises create a strong, trust-based relationship with their customers.

2. Immediate Resolution of Problems

Another critical expectation customers have is quickly resolving any issues they encounter. When problems arise, customers want to feel assured that the business will address their concerns promptly and effectively.

Responsiveness is key. Customers appreciate when businesses acknowledge their complaints quickly and take immediate steps to resolve the issue. This responsiveness solves the immediate problem and demonstrates the business's commitment to customer satisfaction. It shows that the company values its customers' time and concerns.

Empathy and action are also essential. When addressing customer complaints, businesses should focus on solving the problem and show genuine concern for the customer's experience. This means listening carefully to the customer's concerns, apologizing when necessary, and keeping the customer informed throughout the resolution process. Even if the outcome is unsatisfactory, the customer will appreciate the effort and transparency.

3. Genuine Empathy When Things Go Wrong

Empathy is a powerful tool in customer service. Customers expect businesses to respond with genuine empathy and understanding when things go wrong. This goes beyond simply resolving the issue; it involves acknowledging the customer's feelings and showing that the business cares about their experience.

Empathy involves actively listening to the customer's concerns and validating their feelings. For instance, if a customer is frustrated with a defective product, the business should acknowledge the inconvenience and express genuine regret for the situation. This human touch can significantly affect how the customer perceives the interaction.

Body language and tone also matter. Customers often gauge empathy through non-verbal cues. A warm, understanding tone of voice and appropriate body language can convey empathy and reassure the customer that their concerns are being taken seriously. When customers feel understood and valued, they are more likely to forgive mistakes and remain loyal to the business.

4. Recognition and Knowledge of the Customer

Customers appreciate being recognized and valued as individuals. Personalization in customer service can significantly enhance the customer experience and foster loyalty.

Using customer names is a simple yet effective way to show recognition. Addressing customers by their first name during interactions creates a more personal and engaging experience. It makes customers feel valued and acknowledged.

Personalized experiences go beyond just using names. Businesses that remember customers' preferences, past purchases, and specific needs can provide more tailored and relevant service. For example, a restaurant that remembers a regular customer's favorite dish or a retailer that recommends products based on previous purchases can create a more personalized and satisfying experience.

Building relationships is about more than just transactions. Businesses should aim to build genuine relationships with their customers. This involves regular check-ins, personalized communications, and creating opportunities for customers to provide feedback. By showing that they care about the customer's overall experience, businesses can create a loyal customer base that feels valued and connected to the brand.

Implementing Systems for Enhanced Customer Service

To consistently meet these customer expectations, businesses must implement effective systems and processes. Here are some strategies to enhance customer service delivery:

1. Training and Development

Investing in regular training and development for customer service staff is crucial. Employees should be trained in product knowledge, and well-trained employees should be better equipped to handle customer inquiries and complaints effectively.

Role-playing exercises can be particularly useful in training. These exercises allow employees to practice handling different customer scenarios in a controlled environment. By simulating real-life situations, employees can develop the skills and confidence needed to provide excellent customer service.

2. Feedback Mechanisms

Implementing robust feedback mechanisms allows businesses to gather insights directly from customers. This feedback can be used to identify areas for improvement and make necessary adjustments.

Surveys and feedback forms are standard tools for collecting customer feedback. Businesses can use these tools to gather information on customer satisfaction, preferences, and pain points. Analyzing this feedback can help identify trends and areas where the business can enhance its service.

Regular check-ins with customers also provide valuable insights. By contacting customers periodically, businesses can gather real-time feedback and address any emerging issues before they escalate.

3. Technology and Automation

Leveraging technology can significantly enhance customer service delivery. Automated systems can streamline processes, reduce response times, and provide more efficient service.

Customer Relationship Management (CRM) systems are beneficial. These systems allow businesses to manage customer interactions, track customer data, and personalize communications. With a CRM system, businesses can ensure that no customer inquiry falls through the cracks and that all interactions are tracked and managed effectively.

Chatbots and AI can also improve customer service. These technologies can handle routine inquiries, provide instant responses, and allow human agents to focus on more complex issues. Businesses can offer faster and more efficient service by integrating chatbots and AI into their customer service strategy.

5. Proactive Communication

Being proactive in communication can prevent many issues from escalating. Keeping customers informed about their orders, delays, or changes can help manage their expectations and reduce frustration. For instance, if there is a delay in delivery, telling the customer in advance and providing a revised timeline shows respect for their time and builds trust.

Regular Updates: Provide customers with regular updates on the status of their orders or any service changes. This proactive approach can prevent misunderstandings and enhance customer satisfaction.

Transparency: Be transparent about any issues or delays. Honesty and openness can build trust and show customers that the business values their relationship.

6. Building a Customer-Centric Culture

Creating a customer-centric culture within the organization is crucial for delivering excellent customer service. This involves instilling the importance of customer satisfaction in every employee, from top management to frontline staff.

Leadership Commitment: Leadership should demonstrate a commitment to customer service excellence. By prioritizing customer satisfaction and leading by example, leaders can inspire employees to follow suit.

Employee Empowerment: Empower employees to make decisions that benefit the customer. Providing the authority and tools needed to address customer issues quickly and effectively can enhance service delivery.

Recognition and Rewards: Recognize and reward employees who go above and beyond to deliver exceptional customer service. This not only motivates employees but also reinforces the importance of customer satisfaction.

7. Leveraging Customer Data

Using customer data effectively can help businesses understand their customers better and provide more personalized service. Collecting and analyzing data on customer behavior, preferences, and feedback can provide valuable insights for improving service.

Data Analysis: Analyze customer data to identify trends and patterns. This can help understand customer needs and preferences, allowing for more targeted and effective service strategies.

Personalized Marketing: Use customer data to create customized marketing campaigns. Tailoring marketing messages and offers to individual customers can increase engagement and loyalty.

Predictive Analytics: Utilize predictive analytics to anticipate customer needs and proactively address potential issues. For example, if data shows that a customer is likely to need a product refill, reaching out before they run out can enhance their experience.

8. Creating a Feedback Loop

Establishing a continuous feedback loop between the business and its customers is essential for ongoing improvement. This involves collecting feedback, acting on it, and communicating the changes to the customers.

Feedback Channels: Provide multiple channels for customers to give feedback, such as surveys, social media, and direct communication. Make it easy for customers to share their thoughts and experiences.

Act on Feedback: Use customer feedback to improve products and services. Demonstrating that feedback is valued and acted upon can strengthen customer relationships.

Close the Loop: Inform customers about the changes made based on their feedback. This shows that their opinions matter and that the business is committed to continuous improvement.

Case Studies: Real-World Examples of Excellent Customer Service

Case Study 1: Zappos

Zappos, an online shoe and clothing retailer, is renowned for its exceptional customer service. Their commitment to customer satisfaction is evident in their policies, such as free shipping and returns, a 365-day return policy, and 24/7 customer support. Zappos empowers its employees to go above and beyond for customers, creating memorable experiences that foster loyalty.

For instance, there have been instances where Zappos customer service representatives have stayed on calls for hours to ensure a customer's issue is resolved. This dedication has earned Zappos a loyal customer base and a reputation for outstanding service.

Case Study 2: Ritz-Carlton

The Ritz-Carlton hotel chain is another example of a company that excels in customer service. They follow the motto, "We are Ladies and Gentlemen serving Ladies and Gentlemen," emphasizing the importance of treating customers with utmost respect and care. The Ritz-Carlton empowers its employees to spend up to $2,000 per guest to resolve any issues without needing managerial approval.

This empowerment allows employees to address customer concerns immediately, creating a seamless and satisfying experience. The Ritz-Carlton's commitment to exceptional service has resulted in high customer loyalty and numerous industry accolades.

The key to attracting and keeping customers is understanding and meeting their expectations. Clear brand promises, immediate problem resolution, genuine empathy, and personalized recognition are essential to excellent customer service. You can significantly enhance customer service delivery by adopting a customer-centric mindset, being proactive, empowering your team, fostering continuous improvement, and embracing technology.

Excellent customer service is not about doing one big thing right but consistently doing many little things well. By focusing on these mindset hacks and building robust systems, you can create a loyal customer base that returns and advocates for your business. In the end, it's the genuine connections and positive experiences that make customers come back, transforming them into lifelong patrons.

Chapter 6

TWELVE (12) BEST WAYS TO KEEP CUSTOMERS COMING BACK

The previous chapter explored what customers expect from us as business owners. Now, let's dive into what we must do to meet these expectations and ensure customers return. While many businesses focus on attracting new clients, it's just as vital, if not more so, to nurture the relationship with existing customers. Loyal customers are the backbone of any business, and with the power of social media, they can become your most effective promoters. A loyal customer doesn't just pay for your products or services; they also spread the word about your business to others.

Taking returning customers for granted is a mistake. Customers can come and go, sometimes disappearing without explaining why they're not returning. Protect your investment in earning their trust by taking the best care of them once they are part of your customer base.

Here are twelve strategies to grow your returning customer base.

1. Know Your Customers

Understanding what your customers want is crucial to serving them well. Customers generally look for quality, fair pricing, convenience, prompt services, and confidentiality, all tailored to their personal needs. Take the time to get to know each customer individually. This means collecting and analyzing customer data to understand their preferences, behaviors, and feedback. Utilize this information to offer personalized experiences and products that meet their specific needs.

Why Knowing Your Customers is Important

Knowing your customers allows you to create a more personalized and engaging experience, which is crucial to building loyalty and ensuring repeat business. Customers who feel understood and valued are likelier to return and recommend your business to others. This personalized approach also enables you to anticipate customer needs, address their pain points, and exceed their expectations, which can set you apart from competitors.

How to Get to Know Your Customers

1. **Collect Customer Data:**

- **Surveys and Feedback Forms:** Regularly ask customers to fill out surveys or feedback forms to learn about their preferences and satisfaction levels.

- **Purchase History:** Keep track of customers' purchases to understand their preferences and tailor recommendations accordingly.

- **Website and Social Media:** Monitor how customers interact with your website and social media pages to gather insights into their interests.

2. **Use a CRM System:**

    - Implement a Customer Relationship Management (CRM) system to store and manage customer information. This helps you keep track of their interactions, preferences, and feedback in one place.

3. **Engage on Social Media:**

    - Respond to comments and messages on social media. This helps you understand what customers like and don't like about your products or services.

4. **Talk to Your Customers:**

    - Discuss with customers in person or through phone calls and emails to learn more about their needs and expectations.

How to Use Customer Data

1. **Personalize Marketing:**
    - Send tailored emails and offers based on customer preferences and purchase history. This makes customers feel unique and valued.

2. **Recommend Products:**
    - Use customer data to suggest products they might like based on their previous purchases.

3. **Improve Products and Services:**
    - Use feedback to identify areas for improvement and make changes to meet customer needs better.

4. **Create Loyalty Programs:**
    - Design loyalty programs that reward customers for repeat purchases and referrals. Offer exclusive discounts and special incentives to loyal customers.

5. **Enhance Customer Support:**
    - Provide personalized support using customer data to understand their previous interactions and issues. This helps in offering tailored solutions.

Simple Example

Imagine you run a small bakery. You notice that a customer named Sarah always buys gluten-free products. You could:

1. **Collect Data:** Keep a record of Sarah's purchases and preferences.//
2. **Use CRM:** Store this information in a simple CRM system.
3. **Engage:** Send Sarah a thank-you email with a special offer on gluten-free products.
4. **Recommend:** Next time Sarah visits, suggest new gluten-free items she might like.
5. **Improve:** Ask Sarah for feedback on your gluten-free range and use her suggestions to improve your products.

By taking these simple steps, you create a personalized experience for Sarah, making her feel valued and more likely to return to your bakery.

Knowing your customers is about consistently collecting and using their data to create personalized experiences. This helps build strong relationships, ensures repeat business, and sets your business apart from competitors. Keep it simple, stay engaged, and always strive to understand and meet your customers' needs.

2. Ensure Your Products/Services Work

Ensuring your gods and services consistently meet or exceed customer expectations is foundational for building trust and satisfaction. No matter how exceptional your customer service may be, it cannot fully compensate for unreliable products or services that fall short of what was promised. Here's why this commitment is crucial and how to effectively achieve it:

Why It's Crucial

1. **Customer Trust and Loyalty:**

   - **Reliability:** Customers expect products to work as intended and services to be performed competently. Meeting these expectations consistently builds trust, which is essential for retaining customers and fostering loyalty.

   - **Consistency:** Customers who receive consistent quality and reliability are more likely to return for future purchases and recommend your business to others.

2. **Brand Reputation:**

   - **Positive Word-of-Mouth:** Satisfied customers are your best advocates. Delivering reliable products/services leads to positive word-of-mouth, significantly enhancing your brand's reputation and attracting new customers.

- **Reduced Risks:** Avoiding product defects or service failures helps mitigate the risks of adverse reviews or reputation damage, which can impact your business's growth and success.

3. **Customer Satisfaction and Retention:**

    - **Minimized Disappointment:** Customers are satisfied and less likely to seek alternatives when they receive what they expect. This increases customer retention rates and reduces churn.

    - **Long-Term Relationships:** Building a reputation for reliability and excellence encourages long-term customer relationships, creating a stable customer base that supports sustainable business growth.

How to Ensure Product Reliability

1. **Quality Assurance:**

    - **Robust Testing:** Implement rigorous testing procedures during product development and manufacturing to identify and rectify potential defects early.

- **Quality Control:** Monitor production processes closely to ensure consistency and adherence to quality standards. Regular inspections and audits are essential.

2. **Supplier Relationships:**

   - **Select Reliable Suppliers:** Choose suppliers known for their commitment to quality and reliability. Establish strong partnerships to maintain consistent access to high-quality materials and components.

   - **Quality Assurance Agreements:** Implement agreements outlining quality requirements and suppliers' expectations to uphold product standards.

3. **Continuous Improvement:**

   - **Feedback Mechanisms:** Establish channels for collecting customer feedbackpo on product performance and satisfaction. Act promptly on feedback to address concerns and make necessary improvements.

   - **Innovation and Adaptation:** Stay abreast of technological advancements and market trends to innovate products continually. Adapt your offerings to meet evolving customer needs and preferences.

How to Ensure Service Excellence

1. **Training and Development:**

    o **Continuous Training:** Invest in training programs for your service team to enhance their skills, knowledge, and customer service abilities.

    o **Service Standards:** Define clear service standards and practices to enable consistency in service delivery across all customer interactions.

2. **Customer-Centric Approach:**

    o **Personalized Service:** Tailor services to meet individual customer preferences and requirements. Understand and anticipate customer needs to deliver customized experiences.

    o **Proactive Communication:** Maintain open communication with customers throughout the service process. Address inquiries, provide updates, and seek feedback to demonstrate reliability and commitment.

3. **Quality Assurance in Services:**

    o **Service Guarantees:** Offer guarantees or warranties to assure customers of your commitment to quality and satisfaction.

Clearly communicate terms and conditions to manage expectations effectively.

- **Performance Metrics:** Establish metrics to measure service performance and customer satisfaction. Use these insights to identify areas for improvement and optimize service delivery.

Example: Ensuring Product Reliability

Imagine you manage a software development company. To ensure your products are reliable:

- **Thorough Testing:** Perform extensive testing phases across the software development lifecycle, such as unit testing, integration testing, and user acceptability testing.

- **Beta Testing:** Engage customers in beta testing phases to gather real-world feedback and identify potential issues before full release.

- **Regular Updates:** Provide timely updates and patches to address bugs or security vulnerabilities, demonstrating your commitment to product reliability and customer satisfaction.

Committing to providing dependable products and exceptional services entails more than just meeting, but exceeding client expectations constantly. By prioritizing quality assurance, continuous improvement, and a customer-centric strategy, you can build a reputation for reliability, trustworthiness, and excellence in your industry. This proactive approach enhances client satisfaction and loyalty and strengthens your brand's position in the marketplace for long-term success.

3. Be Easily Accessible.

After making a sale, it's crucial to ensure customers can easily reach out to you. This means investing resources not only in closing the sale but also in nurturing the relationship over time. A key strategy is to stay active on social media platforms where your customers are present. You show that you value their ongoing support by engaging with them through posts, comments, and messages.

Additionally, consider sending special incentives or discounts to show appreciation for their business. These can be exclusive offers or loyalty rewards encouraging repeat purchases and promoting a sense of belonging.

Regular and meaningful communication is another pillar of post-sale engagement. Sending out informative email newsletters keeps customers updated about your latest products, promotions, or industry insights. The key here is to strike a balance—ensure your messages are purposeful and relevant to their interests, avoiding overwhelming them with unnecessary information.

By prioritizing accessibility and ongoing relationship-building efforts, you enable customer satisfaction and increase the likelihood of repeat business and positive word-of-mouth referrals.

4. Make you and your business memorable:

Creating a memorable experience starts with an excellent first impression and continues with consistently positive interactions. Stay positive even when things go wrong, and ensure every customer interaction is positive. Personal touches, such as birthday calls or attending essential events for high-value customers, can significantly impact the experience. Little gestures can make your business unforgettable.

For example, imagine you manage a hotel. Here's how you could create memorable experiences:

- **Personalized Welcome:** Greet guests by name upon arrival and offer a personalized welcome package tailored to their preferences.

- **Customized Experiences:** Offer personalized amenities based on guest preferences, such as favorite snacks or room preferences.

- **Special Occasion Recognition:** Celebrate birthdays or anniversaries with a complimentary room upgrade, a bottle of champagne, or a special dessert.

5. Appreciate your customers.

Showing genuine appreciation to your customers is not just about politeness; it's a strategic approach to building strong relationships and fostering loyalty. Customers who feel valued and recognized are likelier to continue supporting and recommending your business to others. Here's why appreciation matters and how you can implement it effectively:

Why Appreciation Matters

Building Loyalty: When customers feel appreciated, they develop a sense of loyalty towards your brand. This emotional connection goes beyond product features or pricing, influencing their decision to choose your business repeatedly.

Encouraging Advocacy: Customers who are satisfied and feel appreciated are likelier to tell others about their excellent experiences. Word-of-mouth recommendations can significantly impact your business's reputation and attract new customers organically.

Enhancing Customer Satisfaction: Appreciation contributes to overall customer satisfaction by demonstrating that their relationship with your business is valued. It helps in fostering a positive customer experience and building long-term relationships.

Strategies for Showing Appreciation

1. Personalized thank-you: Express gratitude through personalized messages or thank-you notes. Address customers by name and mention specific interactions or purchases, highlighting their importance to your business.

Example: Send a personalized email thanking a consumer for their purchase. Include a sincere appreciation for their support and a discount code for their next purchase as a token of gratitude.

2. Special Rewards and Incentives: Reward loyal customers with meaningful incentives such as discounts, exclusive offers, or early access to new products/services. Recognize customers who refer new business or make repeat purchases.

Example: Implement a loyalty program where customers earn points for every purchase. Offer rewards like a free product/service after accumulating a certain number of points or additional points for referrals and positive reviews.

3. Acknowledging Feedback and Complaints: Demonstrate that customer feedback is valued by actively listening and responding promptly. Address complaints professionally and use feedback to improve your products/services.

Example: If a customer provides feedback about an issue, respond promptly with a personalized message acknowledging their concerns. Offer a solution or compensation to show commitment to their satisfaction.

Example of Appreciation in Action

Imagine you manage a local bakery:

- **Personalized Thank-Yous:** Include handwritten thank-you notes in customers' takeout orders, expressing gratitude for their patronage and inviting them to visit again soon.

- **Customer Loyalty Program:** Launch a digital loyalty program where customers earn points for every purchase. Offer rewards such as a free pastry after a certain number of visits or a discount on their birthday.

- **Feedback Acknowledgment:** Respond to customer reviews on social media and review sites, thanking them for their feedback. Address any concerns publicly and offer to resolve issues to ensure customer satisfaction.

Appreciating your customers is a strategic way to build lasting relationships and foster loyalty. By showing genuine gratitude through personalized gestures, rewards, and responsive customer service, businesses can create positive customer experiences that lead to continued support and advocacy. Remember, small acts of appreciation can significantly impact customer satisfaction and loyalty.

6. Seek Feedback and Act on It.

Seek Feedback and Act on It Pay attention to customer feedback and proactively ask for their opinions. Use surveys to gather insights about your products and services, then act on the information you receive. Show customers that you value their input by implementing their suggestions and making visible changes based on their feedback. This not only improves your offerings but also strengthens customer trust and loyalty.

Strategies for Seeking and Acting on Feedback

1. Proactive Feedback Collection:

- **Surveys and Questionnaires:** Regularly conduct surveys to gather feedback on different aspects of your business, including product quality, customer service, and overall experience.

- **Feedback Forms:** Set up feedback forms on your website, at checkout, or through email to encourage customers to share their thoughts.

2. Actively Listen and Analyze:

- **Pay Attention to Trends:** Identify recurring themes or patterns in customer feedback to prioritize areas for improvement.

- **Use Data Analytics:** Utilize tools and analytics to analyze quantitative data from surveys and qualitative feedback from customer comments.

3. Implement Changes Based on Feedback:

- **Communicate Changes:** Inform customers about your changes based on their feedback. This shows transparency and reinforces that their input is valued.

- **Follow-Up:** Follow up with customers who provide feedback to let them know how their suggestions have been implemented and thank them for their contribution.

Example of Feedback Implementation

Imagine you manage an online clothing store:

- **Surveys and Feedback Forms:** Send post-purchase surveys to customers asking about their shopping experience, product satisfaction, and suggestions for improvement.

- **Analyzing Feedback:** Identify common themes, such as requests for faster shipping options or more detailed product descriptions.

- **Implementing Changes:** Based on feedback, introduce a new express shipping option for faster delivery and update product descriptions to include more sizing details and fabric information.

Business growth and customer satisfaction need to seek feedback and act on it. By listening to your customers, implementing their suggestions, and communicating changes, you demonstrate your commitment to improving their experience and building lasting relationships. This proactive approach enhances your products and services and strengthens customer trust and loyalty.

7. Keep The Experience Fresh and Relevant.

Getting customers to return isn't guaranteed because they've used your services before. There are so many distractions out there that it's easy for them to forget about you. Whether you sell to regular shoppers or other businesses, staying on their radar is crucial. You should check in with businesses occasionally if you provide services to them. Let them know you appreciate their past business and are ready to help again. It's also essential to give them reasons to choose you again. Keep them updated on new products or improvements you've made. Doing this shows you're constantly improving and looking out for their needs.

In today's crowded market, it's not enough to make a sale and move on. You have to keep reminding customers why they should choose you. Sharing updates and improvements gives them a reason to think of you when they need similar services again. You build stronger relationships by staying in touch and showing that you're evolving with their needs. This makes it more likely they'll return to you instead of trying someone new.

With many options available, businesses must stand out by staying connected and offering ongoing value. Showing customers what's new and how it benefits them keeps your business in mind. Whether you reach out directly or through marketing, staying proactive helps you stay relevant. This keeps your current customers happy and attracts new ones who see your commitment to service.

Businesses can build trust and loyalty by focusing on keeping customers happy and informed. When you show genuine interest in their needs and consistently deliver value, they're more likely to stick with you. In a competitive world where attention is fleeting, staying engaged and improving is the key to long-term success and growth.

8. Have The Right People on The Frontline.

Having the right people to interact with customers is crucial for any business. Even if you have a fantastic product, if the person customers deal with isn't friendly or, worse, is rude, it can drive people away. That's why having the right team members on the frontline is essential. These are the people customers first interact with, so they need to be qualified and capable. They should be friendly, efficient, and able to provide personalized service. This positive interaction can make all the difference in creating a good customer experience and building strong business relationships.

Imagine you walk into a store or call a company for help. The first person you talk to sets the tone for your whole experience. If they're helpful and polite, it makes you feel valued as a customer. On the other hand, if they're dismissive or unhelpful, it can leave a wrong impression. Businesses need team members who understand this and can positively engage customers. This keeps customers satisfied and encourages them to return because they know they'll be treated well.

Friendly and efficient service isn't just a bonus—it should be the standard. When customers feel welcomed and respected, they're more likely to trust and recommend the business to others. This is how good business relationships are built and sustained over time. Businesses that prioritize hiring and training frontline staff who excel at customer interaction are investing in their success. They understand that every interaction counts and that a positive customer experience can result in long-term loyalty and growth.

Choosing the right people for the frontline isn't just about skills; it's about attitude and personality, too. Customers appreciate sincerity and genuine care. It shows when team members genuinely enjoy helping customers and solving their problems. These kinds of interactions leave a lasting impression and make customers feel valued. Businesses that consistently deliver this level of service are more likely to stand out in a competitive market and thrive.

Having friendly, efficient, and personalized service from frontline staff is vital for business success. They are the face of the company and play an essential role in influencing client perceptions. By hiring and training the right people, businesses can ensure positive customer experiences that lead to stronger relationships and continued growth.

9. Train, Train, Train!

Investing in continuous training for your staff, both new hires and seasoned employees, is crucial for maintaining high customer service standards and adapting to evolving industry practices. Here's why ongoing training is essential and how you can effectively implement it:

Importance of Continuous Training

Adapting to Change: In today's dynamic business environment, industry practices, and customer expectations evolve rapidly. Regular training ensures your staff remains current with best practices and trends, enabling them to deliver exceptional service.

Improving Customer Satisfaction: Well-trained employees provide more efficient service, resolve issues effectively, and create positive customer experiences. This leads to increased customer satisfaction and loyalty.

Employee Engagement and Retention: Training programs demonstrate your commitment to employee development, boosting morale and job satisfaction. Engaged employees are likelier to stay with your company and contribute to its success.

Strategies for Effective Training

1. Tailored Training Programs:

- **Identify Specific Needs:** Assess each department or team's skills and knowledge gaps.
- **Customize Content:** Tailor training sessions to address specific challenges or opportunities relevant to different roles.

2. Utilizing Internal Expertise:

- **Identify Key Employees:** Tap into the expertise of senior staff or top performers who excel in customer service.
- **Peer Learning:** Encourage employee knowledge sharing and mentorship to foster a learning culture.

3. Leveraging External Resources:

- **External Training Providers:** Bring industry experts or external trainers with fresh perspectives and specialized knowledge.

- **Online Training Platforms:** Utilize e-learning platforms and webinars to deliver flexible and cost-effective training options.

4. Continuous Improvement Approach:

- **Regular Reviews:** Evaluate training effectiveness and gather feedback from staff to refine and improve future programs.

- **Stay Updated:** Stay informed about industry trends and customer feedback to update training content accordingly.

Example of Effective Training Implementation

Imagine you manage a retail chain:

- **Departmental Training:** Conduct separate training sessions for sales associates focusing on product knowledge and customer engagement techniques.

- **Role-Specific Training:** Provide managerial staff leadership and conflict resolution training to enhance team management skills.

- **External Workshops:** Arrange workshops with industry experts to educate staff on trends in upcoming retail and customer service innovations.

Continuous training is a strategic investment that benefits both employees and customers alike. By prioritizing ongoing education, adapting training to meet specific needs, and leveraging internal and external expertise, businesses can enhance customer satisfaction, improve employee retention, and establish long-term success in a competitive market.

10. Collaborate.

Collaborating with customers goes beyond just selling products—it's about working together on meaningful projects that benefit everyone, including the community. By involving customers in activities both inside and outside your business, you can create a positive impact that enhances their experience and strengthens your relationship.

One way to collaborate is by co-creating solutions or developing new products together. This means inviting customers to share their ideas and feedback during the product development. Listening to their input allows you to create products that fit their needs and preferences better. This collaborative approach improves product quality and promotes a sense of ownership and satisfaction among customers, knowing they played a role in its creation.

Another way to engage customers is through pilot testing of new products. This involves giving customers early access to test new offerings and providing feedback before launching them. Their insights can help identify potential issues, refine features, and ensure the product meets expectations. Customers appreciate involvement in this process as it shows their opinions matter and can influence decisions.

Creating online communities is also effective for gathering valuable insights and fostering collaboration. These communities serve as platforms where customers can connect, share experiences, and provide feedback. Businesses can use these insights to improve products, address concerns, and strengthen customer loyalty. Engaging customers in this way builds a sense of belonging and encourages ongoing interaction and support for the brand.

Furthermore, businesses can collaborate with customers on community initiatives and charitable activities. For example, donating a portion of sales to a nonprofit organization or organizing collections for local food banks. By involving customers in these efforts, you contribute to worthy causes and align your brand with values that resonate with your customer base. This builds goodwill and enhances the overall reputation of your business within the community.

Collaborating with customers on various initiatives—whether it's co-creating products, gathering feedback, building online communities, or participating in charitable activities—strengthens relationships and adds value beyond transactions. It demonstrates a commitment to mutual benefit and shared values, fostering loyalty and long-term engagement. Businesses embracing this collaborative approach can differentiate themselves in the market and create lasting positive impacts for their customers and communities.

11. Follow Up.

Following up with customers after they make a purchase is crucial for maintaining their satisfaction and ensuring they feel valued by your business. It's natural for people to sometimes question their decisions after buying something, so proactive follow-up helps to address any concerns and reinforce their confidence in choosing your product or service.

Offering after-sales services is a vital part of this process. This could include installation assistance, troubleshooting support, or warranty information. By providing these services, you show customers that their relationship with your business extends beyond the initial transaction. This builds trust and reassures them that you're committed to their satisfaction even after they've made a purchase.

Giving helpful tips for using the product effectively is another way to support customers post-purchase. This could involve sharing maintenance advice, usage techniques, or ways to get the most out of the product. Such tips enhance their experience and demonstrate your expertise and willingness to help them succeed with their purchase.

Moreover, addressing customer complaints promptly and effectively is crucial. When customers express dissatisfaction or encounter issues, following up with supportive solutions shows that you care about their experience. This can transform a potentially harmful situation into a positive one, fostering loyalty and goodwill. It's about listening to their concerns, taking them seriously, and taking action to resolve them promptly.

Demonstrating genuine care through follow-up actions is essential for building long-term customer loyalty. It's about more than just making a sale—it's about nurturing relationships and showing customers that their satisfaction matters. Businesses prioritizing customer support and after-purchase follow-up are likelier to create positive experiences that keep customers returning. This approach helps avoid buyer remorse and strengthens your reputation as a customer-centric business in a competitive market.

12. Create Loyalty Programs:

Reward programs are designed to reward customers for their loyalty, encouraging them to return and continue doing business with a company. These programs offer incentives, rewards, or unique benefits tailored to different customer behaviors, such as early purchases, repeat buying, or referrals. By customizing rewards based on these actions, businesses can reinforce positive behaviors and build stronger relationships with their customer base.

One way loyalty programs work is by tailoring rewards around specific customer actions. For instance, offering benefits to early bird customers who make purchases soon after a product launch or giving incentives to those who consistently choose your services. By recognizing and rewarding these behaviors, businesses encourage repeat purchases and show appreciation for customer loyalty.

Moreover, loyalty programs effectively gather valuable customer data and demographics. By enrolling customers in these programs, businesses can get information about their preferences, buying habits, and contact details. This data helps better understand customer needs and enables targeted marketing strategies that resonate with specific customer segments.

Exclusive events and early access opportunities are other perks of loyalty programs. Businesses can host special events like meet-and-greets or grant early access to new products or services. These experiences make customers feel valued and privileged, strengthening their connection to the brand and enhancing loyalty.

Additionally, loyalty programs often include special recognition and surprise rewards. This could range from personalized thank-you notes to free or discounted purchase upgrades. These gestures go beyond transactional benefits, creating memorable moments that deepen customer loyalty and satisfaction.

Ultimately, Loyalty programs benefit both clients and businesses alike. Customers enjoy incentives and rewards for their continued patronage, while businesses gain higher retention rates, increased sales, and access to valuable customer insights.

PART TWO

UNDERSTANDING CUSTOMER-SPECIFIC NEEDS AND TRIGGER MOMENTS

Chapter 7

KNOW YOUR CUSTOMER JOURNEY

Understanding and mapping out your customer's journey is essential for providing outstanding customer experiences that meet and exceed expectations.

Each customer interaction with your business marks a unique journey from the initial contact to post-purchase engagement. Companies can refine their strategies to enhance customer satisfaction and loyalty by comprehending these stages and touchpoints.

Here is a guide to help you understand customer expectations at each stage of the customer journey:

Mapping Out the Customer Journey and Touchpoints

1. **Awareness Stage**

Objective: Create brand awareness and provide information.

Customer Expectations: At this initial stage, potential customers discover your brand. They seek clear and concise information to understand what your business offers.

Strategies to Meet Expectations:

- **Website:** Ensure your website is informative, user-friendly, and optimized for search engines.

- **Social Media:** Practice active and engaging social media presence that reflects your brand's values and offerings.

- **Content Marketing:** Use blogs, videos, and infographics to educate and attract your target audience.

- **Advertising:** Invest in both online and offline advertising to increase brand visibility.

2. **Consideration Stage**

Objective: Provide detailed product or service information and build trust.

Customer Expectations: Here, customers compare your offerings with competitors. They seek detailed information about your products or services to make informed decisions.

Strategies to Meet Expectations:

- **Product Details:** Offer comprehensive information about product features, benefits, and pricing on your website.

- **Customer Reviews:** Showcase testimonials and reviews to build credibility.

- **Comparison Tools:** Provide comparison charts and guides to help customers evaluate your products against competitors.

- **Webinars and Demos:** Host live or recorded demonstrations to highlight the value of your products or services.

3. **Purchase Stage**

Objective: Facilitate a smooth and secure transaction.

Customer Expectations: Customers expect a seamless, convenient, and secure buying experience.

Strategies to Meet Expectations:

- **User-Friendly Checkout:** Simplify the checkout process with clear steps and minimal form fields.

- **Payment Options:** provide multiple payment methods, including credit cards, PayPal, and other popular options.

- **Security:** Provide the highest level of protection for online transactions to protect customer data.

- **Support:** Provide accessible customer support via chat, email, or phone to assist with any issues during the purchase.

4. **Post-Purchase Stage**

Objective: Deliver on promises and provide excellent customer support.

Customer Expectations: Customers expect reliable delivery and responsive customer service for questions or issues after purchasing.

Strategies to Meet Expectations:

- **Order Tracking:** Provide real-time order tracking information.

- **Customer Service:** Offer multi-channel support (email, phone, chat) and ensure quick response times.

- **Follow-Up:** Send follow-up emails to confirm delivery and gather feedback on the purchase experience.

- **Problem Resolution:** Address any issues promptly and effectively to maintain customer satisfaction.

5. **Loyalty Stage**

Objective: Foster long-term relationships and encourage repeat business.

Customer Expectations: Loyal customers expect personalized experiences, rewards, and ongoing engagement.

Strategies to Meet Expectations:

- **Personalized Recommendations:** Utilize data analytics to provide personalized product suggestions based on previous purchases.

- **Loyalty Programs:** Implement loyalty programs that reward returning customers with discounts, points, or exclusive offers.

- **Engagement:** Maintain active engagement through social media, email newsletters, and community events.

- **Feedback Loop:** Continuously gather and act on customer feedback to improve products and services.

Identifying and Enhancing Touchpoints

1. **Initial Contact:**

- Ensure that your marketing materials and advertisements are eye-catching and informative.
- Optimize your website for easy navigation and quick access to information.

2. **Engagement:**

    - Use engaging content and interactive elements on your website and social media.
    - Offer valuable content that addresses customer pain points and interests.

3. **Transaction:**

    - Streamline the checkout process and ensure it is mobile-friendly.
    - Provide clear communication during the purchase process, including order confirmations and updates.

4. **After-Sales Support:**

    - Ensure your customer service team is adequately trained and empathetic.
    - Provide easy access to support channels and self-service options.

5. **Building Trust:**

- Transparency: Be honest about your goods and services, including any potential limitations.

- Consistency: Deliver consistent quality and service at every touchpoint.

- Engagement: Show appreciation through personalized communications and rewards.

Businesses can build meaningful and lasting relationships with their customers by thoroughly understanding and optimizing each customer journey stage. This approach meets customer expectations and builds trust and loyalty, ensuring customers return.

Chapter 8

ADDRESS THEIR PAIN POINTS AND OPPORTUNITY FOR IMPROVEMENT

Addressing customers' pain points and identifying opportunities for improvement is essential for businesses to enhance their customer experience and increase customer satisfaction. This chapter outlines a comprehensive approach to understanding and resolving customer issues, thereby fostering long-term loyalty and business growth.

Step 1: Gather Feedback from Customers

The first step to identifying pain points and improvement areas is to gather customer feedback. This can be done through various channels, such as surveys, customer reviews, and social media interactions. Listening to your clients will guide you in understanding their experiences and identify areas where your business can improve. Sometimes, customers even give feedback without the business owner asking for it. Feedback here can be negative or positive. It is essential to pay attention to both and improve the negative feedback significantly.

- **Surveys**: Use online surveys to ask specific questions about customer experiences. Ensure the surveys are concise and easy to complete to encourage higher response rates.

- **Customer Reviews**: Monitor reviews on platforms like Google and product-specific review sites. Reviews often provide detailed insights into customer experiences.

- **Social Media**: Interact with clients on social media platforms. Customers often share their thoughts and experiences freely on these channels.

- **Direct Feedback**: Encourage direct feedback through email, live chat, and customer service calls. Personal interactions can yield in-depth insights.

Step 2: Analyze Customers' Feedback

After gathering feedback, it's essential to analyze the data to identify patterns and trends. This can enable you to identify common pain points and areas where your business can improve. For example, if many customers complain about the same issue, such as slow response times, it may be an opportunity to enhance your customer service. The rule here is to pay attention to what they are saying and what they are not saying.

- **Data Aggregation**: Compile feedback from all sources into a single database for easier analysis.

- **Identify Patterns**: Look for recurring themes and issues in the feedback. This can highlight systemic problems that need addressing.

- **Customer Segmentation**: Break down the feedback by customer segments to understand if certain groups are experiencing specific issues.

- **Sentiment Analysis**: Use tools to analyze the tone and sentiment of the feedback to gauge overall customer satisfaction.

Step 3: Prioritize Improvements

This cannot be overemphasized. What is the essence of feedback when action will not be taken? After identifying areas for improvement, it's important to prioritize them based on their impact on the customer experience and the business. Concentrate on the upgrades that will significantly affect customer satisfaction and business growth.

- **Impact Assessment**: Assess the possible impact of each identified issue on customer satisfaction and business performance.

- **Cost-Benefit Analysis**: Consider the costs involved in addressing each pain point versus the benefits of resolving it.

- **Customer Impact**: Prioritize issues that affect a large number of customers or those that significantly impact the customer journey.

- **Quick Wins vs. Long-Term Fixes**: Balance quick fixes that can immediately improve customer experience with long-term solutions that address root causes.

Step 4: Develop a Plan of Action

Once you have prioritized improvements, develop an action plan to deal with customer pain points and improve the customer experience. This can include setting goals, assigning responsibilities, and establishing timelines for implementation. More importantly, carry out your action plan.

- **Set Clear Goals**: Explain what success looks like for each improvement initiative. Set measurable targets to track progress.

- **Assign Responsibilities**: Ensure that specific team members are accountable for each action item.

- **Timelines**: Create realistic timelines for implementation, considering the complexity of the issues and the resources available.

- **Monitoring and Evaluation**: Regularly review progress against the plan and adjust as needed to stay on track.

Step 5: Communicate with Customers

Communication is vital in addressing customer pain points and improving the customer experience. Communicating with customers about your changes and how they will benefit from them is essential. This can help to create trust and strengthen your relationship with your customers. Do also let them know you acknowledge their pain points and that it is being addressed or have been addressed.

- **Transparent Updates**: Keep customers informed about your steps to address their concerns. Use newsletters, social media updates, and direct communications.

- **Highlight Benefits**: Explain how the changes will improve their experience and solve their issues.

- **Acknowledge Feedback**: Show appreciation for their feedback and acknowledge their role in helping improve your services.

- **Follow-Up**: After implementing changes, follow up with customers to ensure their issues have been resolved and to gather additional feedback.

The Benefits of Addressing Pain Points and Identifying Opportunities

By addressing customer pain points and identifying areas for improvement, you can enhance the customer experience and increase customer satisfaction. This can lead to:

- **Improved Customer Loyalty**: Satisfied customers are more likely to return and recommend your business to others.

- **Increased Revenue**: Happy customers spend more and contribute to higher lifetime value.

- **Better Reputation**: Positive customer experiences lead to good reviews and a strong brand reputation.

- **Continuous Improvement**: Regularly addressing pain points fosters a culture of continuous improvement within your organization.

Addressing customer pain points and identifying opportunities for improvement is a continuous process that requires dedication and proactive management. By systematically gathering and analyzing feedback, prioritizing actions, and communicating effectively with customers, businesses can significantly improve their customer experience for long-term success.

Chapter 9

HANDLING CUSTOMER TRIGGER MOMENTS

Trigger moments are critical in the customer journey, where customers have specific needs to be met to ensure a positive experience. Understanding these needs and providing tailored solutions can assist businesses to improve the customer experience and increase customer satisfaction.

Here are some steps to help you understand customer-specific needs during trigger moments:

Identifying Trigger Moments

The first step in addressing customer-specific needs is pinpointing the trigger moments in their journey. These are instances where customers are likely to require immediate attention or specific solutions. Examples of trigger moments include:

- **Product Search:** When a customer looks for a particular product or service.

- **Inquiry:** When a customer has a question or concern about a product, service, or policy.

- **Issue Resolution:** When a customer faces a problem that needs to be resolved quickly.

- **Purchase Decision:** When a customer is at the decision-making stage of buying a product or service.

- **Post-Purchase:** When a customer needs support after purchasing, such as installation, usage guidance, or troubleshooting.

Identifying these moments is crucial as they represent opportunities to solidify customer satisfaction or risk losing their trust.

Gathering Data

Gathering comprehensive data is essential to understand and respond to customer needs during trigger moments. This data can be sourced from:

- **Surveys:** Collect direct feedback from customers about their experiences and expectations.

- **Customer Reviews:** Analyze reviews to identify common issues and positive feedback.

- **Social Media Interactions:** Monitor and track social media platforms for customer sentiments and engagement.

- **Customer Support Records:** Examine support tickets and interaction logs for patterns in customer issues and resolutions.

- **Website Analytics:** Track customer behavior on your website to identify common pain points and areas of interest.

Collecting and analyzing data can help businesses with essential insights into client behavior and preferences.

Segmenting Customers

Once sufficient data has been gathered, the next step is to segment customers based on their behaviors, interactions, and specific needs. This segmentation can be done using various criteria, such as:

- **Demographics:** Age, gender, location, etc.

- **Behavioral Patterns:** Purchase history, browsing habits, engagement levels.

- **Psychographics:** Interests, values, lifestyle preferences.

- **Customer Value:** High-value vs. low-value customers.

Consumer segmentation enables organizations to better customize their approaches and solutions to the specific needs of distinct consumer groups.

Developing a Plan of Action

Armed with data and segmented customer groups, businesses can now create an action plan to address customer needs during trigger moments. This plan may include:

- **Personalized Recommendations:** Offer products or services based on customer preferences and behavior.

- **Targeted Promotions:** Offer discounts or special deals tailored to specific customer segments.

- **Enhanced Customer Service:** Provide dedicated support channels or personalized assistance for high-value customers.

- **Proactive Engagement:** Based on predictive analysis, reach out to customers before encountering issues.

The plan should be designed to anticipate and address customer needs swiftly and effectively.

Implementing and Evaluating

Once the plan is developed, it must be implemented and continuously evaluated for effectiveness. This involves:

- **Monitoring Customer Feedback:** Regularly check feedback channels to gauge customer satisfaction.

- **Analyzing Customer Behavior:** Use analytics tools to monitor customer behavior and interaction changes.

- **Adjusting Strategies:** Make necessary adjustments to the plan based on feedback and performance metrics.

- **Training Staff:** Ensure employees are well-trained to handle trigger moments and implement the plan effectively.

By regularly evaluating and refining the plan, businesses can ensure that they are consistently serving the customer's needs and improving the overall customer experience.

Handling Customer Anger

An essential aspect of managing trigger moments is effectively handling customer anger, which can arise during these critical points. Understanding the types of anger and appropriate responses is crucial:

- **Frustration:** Customers may feel frustrated due to unmet expectations or prolonged issues. Address this by listening empathetically and providing swift solutions.

- **Disappointment:** When a product or service doesn't meet promised standards, acknowledge the shortfall and offer a sincere apology and corrective action.

- **Confusion:** Customers are confused by complex processes or unclear information and need clear explanations and guidance.

- **Betrayal:** Customers feeling betrayed by perceived dishonesty or unfair treatment require transparent communication and restitution.

By understanding and addressing customer-specific needs during trigger moments, businesses can significantly enhance the customer experience and foster long-term loyalty. This involves identifying key moments, gathering and analyzing data, segmenting customers, developing and implementing tailored plans, and continuously evaluating and refining these strategies. By doing so, businesses can turn critical moments into opportunities to build more robust, loyal customer relationships.

Chapter 10

TYPES OF CUSTOMER ANGER AND POTENTIAL WAYS TO ADDRESS THEM

In any business, customer anger is an inevitable occurrence. However, understanding the root causes of this anger and knowing how to address it effectively can turn a negative situation into an opportunity to build stronger customer relationships. This chapter explains the various types of customer anger and provides strategies for addressing them, ensuring customers feel heard, respected, and valued.

Frustration

Frustration is one of the most common types of customer anger and typically arises from issues such as long wait times, poor service quality, or unclear policies. This anger manifests when customers feel their time or efforts are not respected.

How to Address Frustration:

1. **Empathize with the Customer:**
    - Listen actively to their concerns without interrupting.
    - Show genuine concern for their situation.
    - Use empathetic statements like, "I understand how this must be frustrating for you."

2. **Provide Clear Explanations:**
    - Offer detailed explanations about what caused the issue.
    - Be transparent about any delays or problems.

3. **Offer Apologies:**
    - A sincere apology can go a long way in defusing frustration.
    - Ensure the apology is genuine and not just a formality.

4. **Proactive Solutions:**
    - Provide immediate solutions or alternatives.
    - Follow up to ensure the problem has been resolved to the customer's satisfaction.

By empathizing, explaining, and providing prompt solutions, businesses can change a dissatisfied customer into a loyal one.

Disappointment

Disappointment occurs when customers have high expectations that are not met. This can happen when a product does not meet its standards or service falls short of what was promised.

How to Address Disappointment:

1. **Acknowledge the Disappointment:**
    - Validate their feelings by acknowledging the gap between their expectations and the reality.
    - Use phrases like, "I see this didn't meet your expectations."

2. **Apologize for Shortcomings:**
    - Apologize for any mistakes or unmet promises.
    - Ensure the apology is specific to the customer's complaint.

3. **Offer Solutions:**
    - Provide remedies such as product replacements, service corrections, or refunds.

- Suggest alternatives that might better meet their needs.

4. **Provide Incentives:**

    - Offer discounts, coupons, or other incentives to rebuild trust.
    - Ensure the incentive is perceived as a gesture of goodwill rather than a mere placation.

Businesses can restore customer trust and satisfaction by addressing disappointment and offering tangible solutions.

Blame

Blame arises when customers feel wronged or mistreated. This anger often involves customers directing their frustration at individuals or the company.

How to Address Blame:

1. **Listen Carefully:**

    - Let the customer fully express their concerns without interrupting.
    - Show that you are taking their complaint seriously.

2. **Avoid Defensiveness:**

    - Resist the urge to defend or justify the company's actions immediately.

- Focus on understanding the customer's perspective.

3. **Take Responsibility:**
    - Acknowledge any mistakes or miscommunications.
    - Offer a sincere apology for any wrongdoing.

4. **Provide Solutions:**
    - Suggest concrete steps to rectify the situation.
    - Ensure follow-through on promised actions to demonstrate commitment to resolving the issue.

Businesses can de-escalate anger and rebuild trust by addressing blame with a non-defensive attitude and a willingness to take responsibility.

Outrage

Outrage is a more intense form of anger that can arise from severe service failures or product defects. This type of anger requires immediate and decisive action.

How to Address Outrage:

1. **Respond Quickly:**
    - Acknowledge the issue immediately.

- Show urgency in addressing the problem.

2. **Acknowledge the Seriousness:**
    - Validate the customer's feelings of outrage.
    - Use robust and empathetic language to show you understand the gravity of the situation.

3. **Provide Clear Solutions:**
    - List out specific steps that will be taken to resolve the issue.
    - Ensure these steps are communicated clearly and followed through.

4. **Remain Calm and Professional:**
    - Maintain a composed demeanor, even if the customer is highly emotional.
    - Show empathy without getting emotionally involved.

By handling outrage with urgency and professionalism, businesses can change a potentially harmful situation into an opportunity to demonstrate exceptional customer service.

Common Triggers of Customer Anger

Customer anger is often triggered by specific experiences, such as:

1. **Being Ignored:**
   - Customers feel undervalued when their concerns are not acknowledged.

2. **Being Tossed Around:**
   - Being transferred between multiple representatives without resolution can increase frustration.

3. **Being Faced with Incompetence:**
   - Poorly trained staff or lack of knowledge can lead to dissatisfaction.

4. **Being Disrespected:**
   - Rude or dismissive behavior from staff can escalate anger quickly.

5. **Being Abandoned:**
   - Failure to fulfill promises or requests leaves customers feeling neglected.

6. **Being Faced with a Cumbersome Process:**
   - Complicated procedures or bureaucratic hurdles can lead to significant frustration.

Reflecting on Personal Experiences

We are all human and may have experienced these triggers in our interactions with other businesses. Reflecting on how these situations made you feel can help you understand your customers' points of view.

The Impact on Business

Making customers angry harms any business, affecting the bottom line and overall reputation. Understanding the different types of customer anger and providing tailored solutions can help businesses effectively address and de-escalate customer anger. Businesses can increase customer loyalty and enhance their reputation by responding empathetically, taking responsibility, and providing clear solutions.

Addressing customer anger requires a thoughtful, empathetic approach. By recognizing the type of anger, validating the customer's feelings, and offering clear, proactive solutions, businesses can turn challenging interactions into opportunities for building lasting customer relationships. Remember, every angry customer is an opportunity to demonstrate exceptional service and turn dissatisfaction into loyalty.

EPILOGUE

SUMMARY OF THE CUSTOMER CODE

Thank you for reading "THE CUSTOMER CODE: Find, Attract and Keep Customers for Life." This book is designed to provide valuable insights into the secrets of attracting customers and ensuring they remain loyal after purchasing.

Humans tend to remember two main scenarios: negative and positive experiences. These experiences shape our relationships with others and our perceptions of businesses. By understanding these dynamics, companies can create lasting and positive customer relationships.

Part One: Attracting Customers

1. The Importance of Customers

- Every business has past, present, and potential customers.

- Customers are the primary source of profit and revenue for any business.

- Meeting client needs is essential for acquiring and retaining customers.

2. The Role of Customer Service

- Customer service encompasses the attention and experience provided to customers before, during, and after purchasing goods and services.

- Excellent customer service delivery leads to increased revenue, higher profit margins, and positive word-of-mouth, attracting more customers at a lower marketing cost.

- Both businesses and customers benefit from high-quality customer service. Revisit this chapter to grasp its importance fully.

3. The Power of Mindset

- A business's mindset often determines how well it can handle its customers.

- Customers are more likely to buy and return when their expectations are met.

- The goal of any business should be to get returning customers, and there are specific strategies to achieve this.

Part Two: Retaining Customers

1. Understanding the Customer Journey

- Each customer's journey is unique, and understanding this journey is vital to providing excellent customer service.

- Businesses must understand customer expectations at each journey stage to deliver a seamless and satisfying experience.

2. Addressing Customer Pain Points

- Customer pain points are critical moments when businesses can demonstrate attentiveness and understanding.

- Identifying and addressing these pain points is essential to improve the overall customer experience.

3. Managing Trigger Moments

- Despite the best efforts, trigger moments—when customers become upset or frustrated—can occur.

- Acknowledging and responding quickly to these moments can help restore customer confidence.

- Trigger moments often arise from specific issues, such as blame, frustration, disappointment, or outrage. During these times, businesses should strive to support customers without compromising their values.

Following the principles outlined in this book, businesses can create a customer-centric approach that attracts new customers and fosters loyalty and long-term relationships. Remember that understanding and addressing your consumers' demands at each stage of their journey is critical to success.

CALL TO ACTION

Yippee...

Thank you for reading to the end!

What is the new thing you are taking away from reading this book?

What is the new idea that you will be practicing going forward?

What is the wrong idea that this book has called your attention to and will be dropping as a bad customer service idea?

When you look within, what are the things you have been practicing that will ensure repeat business?

The Customer Code has defined a clear pathway for keeping customers glued to you and your business. I believe each item will be taken seriously and implemented so we begin to see results in our businesses.

Thank you.

MEET THE AUTHOR

I am Falilat Adeyemi-Salami, a dedicated advocate for enhancing customer service and experience standards for entrepreneurs, business owners, and corporate organisations. My journey began in 2006 when I unexpectedly transitioned from an introverted intern at a reputable financial institution to a Customer Service Officer. This surprising shift challenged me, but I chose to embrace it, striving to excel in my role.

Over the past 16 years, I have transformed this initial challenge into a flourishing career. Today, I am a seasoned professional who writes, teaches, and coaches on the complexities of outstanding customer service. Witnessing poor customer service is disheartening for me, as I am passionate about helping businesses foster loyal and satisfied customers.

I invite you to share insights from The Customer Code with your colleagues, friends, and family. Stay connected with me on social media to benefit from my extensive hands-on experience in customer-centric business environments.

Connect with me:

- **Facebook**: Falilat Adeyemi-Salami
- **Facebook Page**: UPgradeyourservice
- **Instagram**: @lilatadeyemi-salami
- **WhatsApp**: +234 806 729 3565

Together, let's elevate the standards of customer service.

www.ingramcontent.com/pod-product-compliance
Lightning Source LLC
Chambersburg PA
CBHW031431210526
45464CB00005B/2145